Easy Money Management

Personal Finance for Beginners

by

Laurick Ingram

giveandsave365.com

Amazon Store Front

It is easier to give and save a little money first and spend what is left, than to spend money first then give and save what is left.

—Laurick Ingram, Director
Give and Save 365, LLC

Preface

*W.I.I.F.M? Whenever presented with new ideas do
not be afraid to ask: What's in It for Me?*
-The Author

Is this book for you?

Have you been meaning to start a savings

plan for days? Weeks? Months? Years? Do not be

embarrassed, this is a sticking point for many

people for reasons ranging from "I can't afford to

save any money!" to its equally popular cousin,

"I'll get to it when I have time." We all have the

same 24 hours in every day. I'm here to tell you

that you can't afford not to save.

Two great challenges people face when it comes to getting better at managing their money are (1) procrastination and (2) information overload. To overcome the first challenge of procrastination, I have crafted a plan that will allow you to start building good money habits on as little as $1.00 a day ($7.00 a week) given to a good cause and $1.00 a day ($7.00 a week) saved for yourself. That means if you have $2.00 in your pocket, purse, or piggy bank, you can start improving your money skills today. Depending on what you owe or have, this may seem small, but remember that a mustard seed starts out about the size of a pinhead; but plant that seed properly and over time it will grow into a tree. Similarly, if whenever you get money, you can give a little to make someone else's life better and save a little to make your life better, then you can grow your thinking towards good money management. The second challenge is there is so much information—sometimes disinformation—about money that you do not know what to believe. My solution for that was to write a book that is short enough to keep your interest, but long enough to cover what is important.

What is the Give and Save 3-6-5 Concept? At Give and Save 3-6-5, we believe in creating prosperity through philanthropy. We show you how to grow your giving through faith and grow your faith through saving. It takes faith to give without expecting anything in return; therefore, faith grows your giving. As you save and watch your money accumulate and grow, you realize even though you have given money to help others, your own storehouse is increasing as well as your ability to manage it. Therefore, saving grows your faith. I learned this because, during my life, I knew people who would give you the clothes off their back, but they frequently ran into money troubles themselves. On the other hand, I have met people who made good money but were so stingy, they would not give you a dollar for a bottle of water if you were on fire. I concluded the sweet spot for money is somewhere in between helping others and bettering yourselves. This book shows you how to find that sweet spot, but to get there you must decide you want to be there and act accordingly. Don't wait days, weeks, or months. Here and now, you can start using a little of every dollar that comes into your life to help others and better yourself.

For this plan to work, you have to work it. You learn how to ride a bike by getting on and pedaling, not by thinking about doing it or watching someone else do it and wishing you were that person. Take the action steps listed at the end of each chapter. You will be glad you did.

Let's get started!

CONTENTS

Introduction

People, words, decisions, and actions are four critical ingredients needed to change your life.

-The Author

No matter what you want out of life, four things will help you or hinder you from getting those things:

1. The people you know

2. The words you know

3. The decisions you make

4. The actions you take

Before you read another word, ask yourself,

are you

1. willing to meet new people?

2. willing to learn new words?

3. willing to make different decisions?

4. willing to take new actions?

Thank you for buying this book; my family and I appreciate it. But if your answer to the four questions above is no, then you will probably not get much out of this book. You would be better off either returning it (we will give you a full refund) or giving it to a friend who is ready, willing, and open to change.

Conversely, if your answer to the four questions above is yes or even maybe, then congratulations: you have just taken the first step toward a brighter financial future.

Why I Wrote This Book

A wise person learns from his mistakes, but a wiser one learns from somebody else's mistakes.
                                                        -My Brother Harold

I wrote this book both to share with you the reader some of the mistakes I made as well as what I learned from them. Hopefully, you can learn from them without having to make them. The first big one was knowing what to do, but not doing it.

When I was twenty years old, working as a cashier at Quik Mart, I read a book that outlined a great strategy for saving and investing money, written by a guy who began working for $48 a week but retired with a couple million dollars in cash and assets. So, at twenty years old, I knew what to do, but I did not start doing it until twenty-five years later. About ten years after reading that book, I met a woman named Suzy who did a lot of charitable work, including volunteering in Miami Jackson Hospital's neonatal care center. Through Suzy I met her husband, "Mo" Chorney, a silver-haired, handsome guy in his seventies who took a liking to me. For the majority of my life I'd known a lot about working for money but knew little about getting money to work for me. For years Mo tried to teach me about managing money, and for years I did nothing with what he tried to teach me.

Then one day, it hit me. I was sitting in Mo's Florida home, in one of the two mansions he owned on Golden Beach. Mo traveled the world, made sure all of his children lived in beautiful homes, and funded all his grandchildren's college educations. He owned another home in Rhode Island and several rental properties. I, on the other hand, had a great job, but if I lost that job, after six months I would have no savings left. That day I realized that one of us knew a lot about money and one of us did not. I was the one who did not. From that day forward, I began to listen and learn from Mo. (Thank you, Mo, for being patient with me.) More importantly, I decided to not only know but to do. I have heard the best time to plant a tree is twenty- five years ago; the second-best time is now. I could not get those twenty-five years back, so I decided to act where I was. Eight years from that moment, my wife and I were in a position either to continue in our careers or to retire comfortably from those careers and try some new things. We both decided to try some new things, and we have never looked back nor regretted it.

The irony for us was that many of our friends—young and old—were struggling financially. These struggles seemed to cut across race, age, education, religion, and marital status. The struggles took the form of lost jobs, foreclosed homes, no money for college, repossessed cars, skyrocketing medical costs, no health insurance, or being up to their eyeballs in credit card debt.

Since my wife and I have a heart for service, we wanted to help. In many cases, we offered to meet with them, counsel them, and share how we were successful and what mistakes we had made. Maybe one out of ten of the people we talked with listened, and maybe one out of twenty-five decided to change the way they handled their money. This puzzled me because I had trouble understanding how people could spend so much time complaining or even praying about money but little or no time learning about it.

My wife suggested that I was part of the problem—that change scares a lot of people, like it did me when Mo was trying to teach me. Also, she said, the way I explained things was complex and challenged values our friends had held for most of their lives. On top of that was the fact that many people hold fast to opinions more because they are theirs than because they are right.

While I was considering my wife's observations, I attended some budgeting classes where the instructors used detailed spreadsheets to emphasize the need to budget and know where every penny goes. The presentation made sense since the people attending the classes wanted to learn about handling their money better, but I found the idea of tracking every dollar spent to be both complicated and scary, particularly because I (like most people) wasn't in the habit of doing so. This helped me see my wife's point more clearly: If it seems too complicated, most people will do nothing. If it is different from what they are used to, it scares them. I also realized that the few people we counseled who had changed their handling of money were either young adults—who were clearly open to building new habits because their other habits had not had enough time to become cast in stone—or lifetime learners—who were excited about learning and trying new things.

So, back to why I wrote this book. First and foremost, I am a witness that when it comes to money, you can overcome your fears and change your habits. With so much information and misinformation—social media, cable channels, satellite radio, online advertisers—coming at you, it is hard to know where to start and what is true. I designed this book to be short, succinct, and easy to understand. Its principles are demonstrated in small, specific steps. Next, over the years I have known friends, associates, and coworkers who have not read a complete book since they left school. Many of these people are successful in their fields, but for whatever reason, reading an entire book is not something they enjoy or make time for. I enjoy reading, but when I first began learning how to handle money, many of the books were so thick and technical, I could not get through the first few pages before returning them to the library or putting them on my bookshelf as dust collectors. So, what I did was look for books on money that children and young adults could understand. "The shorter, the better" was my motto. This search inspired me to write one of my own. This book is short enough that it can be read in one sitting. If you are one of those people who does not normally read books but are reading this one, at least if someone asks, you can answer honestly that you have read one book this year.

Finally, I wanted to teach some financial skills in a way that was simple enough that they could be learned quickly and applied immediately (rather than waiting twenty-five years like I did). This way, my readers can start succeeding right out of the gate, because nothing fuels success like success. Now, in the words of my eleventh-grade math teacher, Lester Sandoval: "Let us move on!"

Action Steps

$ A Person: Meet one new person, you believe is better at managing money than you are.

$ A Word: Learn one new word about money this week.

$ A Decision: Get two dollars and decide where you will keep the first dollar you are going to save and who you will give your other dollar to.

$ An Action: Now act. Place your first dollar somewhere safe and give the other one away. For example, here is what I did with my first two bills: One (C95951805B), I keep somewhere safe as a reminder of the day I began my new habit. The other (C95951806 B) I gave to New Birth Baptist Church, Miami, Florida.

The Five-Minute Crash Course

It's not just how much you make, it's how much you keep, and how much of what you keep makes more for you.

Maurice "Mo" Chorney

A few years back, my church was holding a youth conference. I was asked to speak at a breakout session designed to teach high school and college-aged students about managing their money. I figured that given everything else going on at the conference, I would have the students' attention for about five minutes. My goal was to create a lesson plan that would not only teach them something about money but enable them to teach that something to someone else. This five-minute crash course is what I came up with. After I explained it to each student, he or she had to explain it back to me. Since then, I've made this my standard spiel whenever talking to young people about money for the first time.

Whenever I run into those that I have taught this to, I ask them if they remember what I taught them. So far everyone has remembered. If you get nothing else out of this book, you will in the next five minutes learn something that can change the course of your financial life. Remember, first learn it, and then do it until it becomes a habit.

For as long as I can remember, my eldest brother Harold loved to quote our grandmother, Victoria McCullough, who said, "If you make a dollar, save a dime." Years later, my pastor, Bishop Victor Curry, taught me, "If you make a dollar, tithe a dime." Because I grew to see the value in both, I taught my sons, Joshua and Jawanza, "When you get a dollar, give a dime and save a dime." If you develop that habit, for every dollar you get, you will know you are enriching your own life as well as the lives of others.

The Five-Minute Crash Course

When it comes to your money, you are doing one of three Gs with it. You are

1. going broke;

2. going into debt; or

3.   getting ahead.

The good news is, if you are not doing the third G, you can start getting ahead today. The affirmation card at the end of this chapter shows you how.

Action Steps

$ Photograph or print the <u>Easy Money Management Five-Minute Crash Course</u> and put it somewhere that you will see it daily. (Mine is on my vision board and a picture of it is in my cell phone.) It will show you how to get to and stay in the third "G" method of managing your money.

$ By putting it where you will see it every day, you are planting it in your mind, where it can take root and grow and blossom into a habit for life. That ends your five-minute crash course on money management. If you want to learn more, then read on, but if you learn and do this one thing, it will change your ideas about money forever. When it comes to your dollars, your new habit, starting today, is to always be getting and staying ahead.

$ Beware of some words. I have already emphasized the importance and power of knowing and using good money words. Conversely, bad money words have power as well. I use the word "broke" to illustrate one of the poor money management habits, but do not use it to describe your financial situation. Just as you can plant seeds of prosperity in your mind, you can plant seeds of poverty. Whichever seed you plant, is going to grow. Words like "broke" and "poor" repel money and opportunities to make money. Right now, commit to never using words like those to describe your finances.

giveandsave365.com

Teaching you how to use every dollar you get to add value to your life and the lives of others.

GIVE AND SAVE 365

THE EASY MONEY MANAGEMENT FIVE-MINUTE CRASH COURSE

© 2017, GiveAndSave365, LLC

1. GOING BROKE HABIT OF MONEY MANAGEMENT

YOU MAKE, GET AN ALLOWANCE, OR GIFT OF	$100
YOU SPEND ON BILLS OR PURCHASES	-$100
YOU HAVE LEFT UNTIL YOU GET MORE	$0

2. GOING INTO DEBT HABIT OF MONEY MANAGEMENT

YOU MAKE, GET AN ALLOWANCE, OR GIFT OF	$100
YOU SPENT ON BILLS OR PURCHASES	-$100
YOU BORROWED	-$10
THE NEXT $100 YOU GET YOU ALREADY OWE	-$10

3. GETTING AND STAYING AHEAD HABIT OF MONEY MANAGEMENT

YOU MAKE, GET AN ALLOWANCE, OR GIFT OF	$100
YOU SPENT ON BILLS OR PURCHASES	-$80
YOU SAVED (YOU PAID YOURSELF FIRST)	$10
YOU GAVE (YOU HELPED SOMEBODY)	$10
YOU HAVE LEFT UNTIL YOU GET MORE	+$10

NAME: _____ DATE: _____

We guarantee you will feel good about what you are doing with your money and what your money is doing for you and others.

19

Why People Go Broke

If to do were as easy as to know what were good to do, chapels had been churches and poor men's cottages princes' palaces

.

-William Shakespeare,
Merchant of Venice

Knowing "ain't" doing!

—Me translating Shakespeare

If a person loses his or her job or has no money coming in to start with, in that case the person needs to get a job, sell something, provide a service, or get an allowance, but he or she somehow must get some money coming in. Believe it or not, that is not the problem I see the most. Most of the people I know who out of their own mouths say they are "broke" are receiving money from some source on a regular basis. If you ask many of them whether they are taking in more money now than they were ten years ago, their answer will usually be yes, yet they are just as broke as they were or have more debt than they did ten years ago. If you are in the habit of being broke, then you will know how to change that after reading this book. But be warned: knowing what to do is easier than doing it. Knowing you need to study for a test is easier than turning off the computer or putting down the cell phone and studying. Knowing you could stand to lose a few pounds is a lot easier than not eating those triple chocolate chunk cookies (I kid you not, those rascals call out to me late at night). Knowing you should give and save money instead of spending it is a lot easier than giving and saving those dollars. How, then, do you make doing these things easy? By deciding to do them and then repeating the action enough until doing it becomes automatic. For example, most people decided a long time ago which hand they would hold their forks in. When they sit down to eat, they do not labor over which hand to use; they grab the fork with the same hand they have used for years and start eating. The reason many people stay broke is they decided a long time ago that they would spend money as fast as they got it. Then they kept doing it until it became as much a habit as how they held their forks.

The goal is to get to where giving and saving 10 percent of all you get becomes automatic. This idea frightens many people. It scares them so much that they end up doing nothing. My goal is for you to start giving and saving today for the next 365 days until it becomes a lifetime habit where, whenever you make a dollar, you automatically give a dime and save a dime.

Action Steps

$ Decide right now that one day this week, you will give at least $7.00 to someone or a cause you care about. It can be the same person or cause each week or a different person or cause.

$ On that same day, save at least $7.00 for yourself. At the end of the year, you will have given $365 and saved $365 for yourself.

$ Now do what you decided and repeat it every week for a year.

How to Not Go into Debt

Everything should be as simple as it can be, but not simpler.
    —Albert Einstein (Attributed)

I will make this as simple as possible. The way to not go into debt is to not go into debt—and if you are already in debt, to not go deeper in debt. If you already owe a family member $20, don't borrow another $20 from a friend or other family member until you pay back the first $20 you borrowed. (Yes, you should pay your family or friends back if you borrowed money from them, and they shouldn't have to remind you.) Few people can afford to buy a car or house using cash; therefore, you will probably have to finance these two big ticket items. As far as everything else goes, pay cash, or if you charge it, pay off your credit card at the end of each month. If you already have balances on your charge card(s), do not charge anything else until you have paid them off. But you say, "I can't start saving until I am out of debt." Wrong!

You just have to treat your dollar a little differently from people who don't have debt. You must give a dime, save a dime, and pay two dimes toward what you owe. You must save, because if you do not save, the first time you need money for something important, you will have to borrow it, and voilà—I have always liked that word—more debt. Also, for every dollar you save, your debt is decreased. For example, if you owe $10 and have $0 saved, your net worth (what you have minus what you owe) is -$10. If you owe $10 but have $1 saved, your net worth is -$9, 10 percent more than before. If you keep saving and growing your money, your net worth will overtake your debt, but more importantly, you will have developed the habit of getting ahead and staying ahead (which I'll discuss in the next chapter).

Action Steps

$ Whatever you owe, you have to pay it back and most likely with interest. Chances are you got in debt by spending more than you could afford. You decided you would borrow money, but now that you borrowed it you have to pay it back.

$ For the next week do not charge anything. Give $7.00 to a person or cause and save $7.00 for yourself. This may seem small, but you cannot grow an apple tree if you never plant the seeds. The energy and possibility of growth exist in those seeds, and when properly planted and cared for they bear fruit. Remember you got into debt by spending more than you could afford. By giving and saving before you spend, you are proving to yourself that you can have more money than you need.

$ Now get through the next week.

Getting Ahead and Staying Ahead

When presenting new ideas, tell your audience what you are going to tell them, tell them, then tell them what you told them.

—Ms. Yvonne Gable,
My High School English Teacher

Getting ahead is a direction, not a destination. The best way to keep going broke or get into more debt is to repeat the habits that got you there and keep you there. The way to get ahead is to decide you want to get ahead and then build the habits that drive you in that direction.

29

At the beginning of this book, I wrote the following:

Before you read another word, ask yourself, are you

1. willing to meet new people?

2. willing to learn new words?

3. willing to make different decisions?

4. willing to take new actions?

To go ahead, get ahead, and stay ahead, your lifetime assignment starting today will be to meet people who use the words, make the decisions, and take the actions that drive them in that direction—people whose conversations include statements like these:

- I paid my sister back the money I

borrowed from her without her having to ask me for it. Yes, you should pay family and friends back money that you borrowed without them having to be reminded by you.

- I paid cash for the new shoes I bought for the party next week.

- All my credit cards are paid off, and if I use one, I pay it off by the end of the month.

- I am going to wait until I can pay cash for a new television before I get it.

- Every two weeks, I put money away for Christmas (or whatever holiday you celebrate) so that I do not have to charge any gifts.

- I volunteer for something or someone I care about.

- I have an automatic deduction plan that puts money into my retirement account.

- I have an automatic savings account for vacations and emergencies.

- Or my personal favorite, I give and save 365 days a year. "But," you say, "I don't get money every day." I understand that, maybe you get money once a week, once a month or once in a while: The point is that every day, you can decide when you get it, to give and save some of it. This way no matter when it comes you are ready.

This book is meant to offer ideas that you can choose to sow into your thoughts until they take hold and grow into action. Emerson said: "Sow a thought and you reap an act; sow an act and you reap a habit; sow a habit and you reap a character; sow a character and you reap a destiny." A bright and great financial destiny awaits you.

The Power of a Dollar A Day

Small things done are better than great things planned.

—Note on a Secretary's Bulletin Board

A long time ago, King Solomon wrote, "Start children off on the way they should go, and even when they are old, they will not turn from it." Many of our money troubles grow out of bad habits we begin when we are young, and they keep repeating until they become like old friends. One aim of this book is to help you start giving and saving as soon as you can in your life—and the sooner, the better.

Robert G. Allen said, "One dollar a day can make you a millionaire or it can bankrupt you. A dollar a day flowing into your life from interest can make you a fortune or it can bankrupt you by flowing out of your life." Here is the proof.

First, if you earned $1 a day for a year, at the end of the year you would have $365. If you spent it all, in forty years you would have nothing—unless what you spent it on lasted forty years, which is unlikely.

Second, if you borrowed $1 a day for one year only, at the end of the year you would have borrowed $365. Let's say you don't have to make any payments for forty years, but the interest rate is 20 percent (the amount some credit card companies charge). In forty years, you would owe a little over a million dollars.

But if you saved $1 a day for one year, at the end of the year you would have $365. If you earned 20 percent on that money over the next forty years, you would have $1,018,623.

That is why a dollar a day flowing into your life can make you a fortune, whereas $1 a day flowing out of your life can bankrupt you. Make sure the dollars are flowing into your life and the lives of others.

A Four-Step Plan: Creating Prosperity Through Philanthropy

If a thousand-mile journey begins with one step, the $10,000 saved begins with one dollar saved.

—The Author

1. Give one dollar a day ($7.00 a week) to whatever church, cause, charity, group, or person you consider worthy.

2. Save one dollar a day ($7.00 a week).

3. Learn and apply one new word about money each week.

4. Repeat

If you follow this plan for one year, you will

have laid a rock-solid foundation upon which to build your financial future. You will be amazed at how these small steps accumulate. Then, once the foundation is laid, you can always give more, save more, and learn more.

If you were to repeat this cycle yearly and invest the $7.00 a week in an investment account with a return of 7.2%, then after 28 years, you would have given away $10,220, but in your investment account, you would have saved $32,768, and in your knowledge bank 1,456 good money words to help you manage your money.

* * *

In his book, *The Magic of Thinking Big,* David J. Schwartz, says, "An only fair idea acted upon, and developed, is 100 percent better than a terrific idea that dies, because it isn't followed up."

There are many good people and plans out there that can help gain and maintain control of your finances; however, they are of little value to you if you never start using them. The small lessons you have learned in this book, if you practice them, are worth far more than the big ideas you never get around to doing. Said another way, a dollar a day saved and invested over time is worth more than the thousands you plan to save but never get around to saving.

Afterword

Give and Save 365, LLC, was founded by my wife and me. The company's core concept is creating prosperity through philanthropy. We believe you can increase your giving through faith, while increasing your faith through saving. Our objective is to teach you how to use every dollar you get to add value to your life and the lives of others.

I agree with Stephen Covey, that teaching something requires a deeper understanding than just learning it. Whatever good things you have learned here, I encourage you not only to develop your own lifetime habit of giving and saving, but also to teach at least one other person what you have learned. All you need to begin is a willing heart and $2.

I close with the parable of the ten birds. If ten birds are sitting on a fence, and one decides to fly away, how many birds are left on the fence? Ten birds are left, because deciding to fly is not the same as flapping your wings and taking off.

I say to you, do not learn this today and then wait twenty-five years to start doing it. Right here, right now, take off!

Thank you for sharing your precious time with us. We would enjoy keeping in contact with you. You can find me, The Give and Save Guy, on LinkedIn, Facebook, Instagram, or Twitter. If you have enjoyed this book, please take a moment to write a review on amazon.com. If there is something you would like to see changed, please contact me directly with your comments and I will get back to you.

God bless!

Acknowledgements

In memory of Arimentha Ingram, my mother, who even on welfare, raising nine children, scraped together enough money to buy me books that taught me the magic of reading.

To the late Harold "Sonny" Ingraham, my brother from another mother. My dear, sweet, brother, God knows I treasure those memories and all that you taught me.

To Kim, my wife and the mother of my children. Mom was right, you were the right one for me.

To my sons, Joshua and Jawanza; you're two of my heroes.

To my brother Ronald, for demonstrating what faith in action looks like.

To my best friend, NBA Scout Irving Thomas, who taught me that talent without work is like a shiny new sports car with no fuel; it may look flashy, but it is not going anywhere.

Special thanks to Armstrong Creative Consulting: Davenya, you and Sam are to Give and Save 365, what icing is to a birthday cake.

About the Author

Laurick is the founder of Give and Save 3-6-5, a company dedicated to teaching people how to add value to their lives and the lives of others. He is the author of the Easy Money Management Guide, Easy Money Management Weekly Journal, Live Life Like a Pro and Student Loan Exit Plan. His last book was a part of his commitment to helping families pay off their student loans early.

His inspiration to focus on student loan debt as a part of his strategy came when he was a guest speaker at a financial literacy seminar. A medical student raised her hand and asked him what she could do about her $240,000 in student loans. He did not have an answer for her, but her question caused him to study the issues facing her and many like her. What he learned was that more than half the families he spoke to had student loan debt. He set out to build a team of people who could help guide people in similar situations and in 2020 he launched Student Loan Exit Plan, a multi-step plan for paying off student loans.

Laurick is a proud mentor for the Miami-Dade County Public Schools 5000 Role Models of

Excellence, and the youngest brother of the late Dr. Robert B. Ingram, one of the original 500 Role Models. In 2018, the United Nations Association (Broward Chapter) honored him for his efforts to eradicate poverty; in 2018, Legacy magazine named him as one of South Florida's "50 Most Powerful Black Leaders in Business & Industry;" he has been interviewed on radio and television as well as mentioned in more than 100 journals and publications.

The End

www.ingramcontent.com/pod-product-compliance
Lightning Source LLC
Chambersburg PA
CBHW050539210326
41520CB00012B/2643